The Christian Family

THE CHRISTIAN FAMILY

by
Thomas van Braam Barrett

MOREHOUSE-GORHAM CO.
New York
1958

PRINTED IN THE UNITED STATES OF AMERICA
BY THE HADDON CRAFTSMEN, INC., SCRANTON, PA.

PREFACE

I AM by no means what might be called an expert on the subject of the Christian family. I am no specialist in psychology, or education, or anything else that is sometimes considered necessary in the equipment of an author writing a book on this complex matter. All I can offer as an apologia for daring to write this essay is my conviction that love, marriage, and the family are not esoteric matters whose meanings are revealed only to specialists. In these relationships we are all specialists. This does not mean that a man who has had two sets of parents and four wives is the most expert marriage counsellor. It does mean that every child and parent, husband and wife, brother and sister do know something of family life, even if all that is known is bad.

"There is a spirit in man: and the inspiration of the Almighty giveth them understanding." So said Elihu, in the Book of Job, speaking to Job's older and more learned friends. The first thing to be said about a Christian, before speaking of Christian families, is that God reveals Himself to every individual who will listen, through the imagination and reason which He has given to them. There are therefore some things a man can know and believe in whether he is a specialist or not.

I will be bold, then, like Elihu, and say I know something about family life. I have read very few books about the family, but I have been a son, a lover, a husband, a father. I have failed in all these things. Perhaps not completely, but noticeably. Therefore I do not write as one who has achieved success. I write as a human being, and, by the grace of God, as a Christian, holding within my memory and experience something of the difficulty, joy, and sadness of family life. I have no formulas to offer. I have no foolproof plan whereby anyone can have a happy Christian family. There is no formula that will meet every contingency.

I am persuaded that the family can achieve its purpose (the by-product of which is a relative kind of happiness) only within the awareness of God, and by His help. I shall begin these chapters with a quotation from the distinguished German theologian Emil Brunner:

Even the Christian and the Christian moralist stand baffled and helpless before many of the problems of marriage. . . . We only need to remind ourselves once more . . . that so long as marriage exists there will be insoluble problems; so long as man lives "in this flesh" he will never finally solve the problem of his sex nature. Even in the ethic of marriage the final word must be: to live on the Divine forgiveness.[1]

If we do not recognize this at the start, all our discussions will be as unreal as a Hollywood set, and our solutions of family problems will be paper solutions with no relevance to the life of a living, suffering, loving, and desiring family.

T.V.B.

[1] From *The Divine Imperative* by Emil Brunner. Copyright, 1947, by W. L. Jenkins, The Westminster Press. Used by permission.

CONTENTS

The Christian Family

Chapter 1

THE PRESENT SITUATION

MOST people in western civilization still believe that the family is the basic unit of social life. Most of us, furthermore, believe in monogamy, and hold it to be preferable to polygamy, or polyandry. It is of course true that polygamy was practised during Old Testament times, and more recently by the Mormons, and it is also true that minority groups of people in this century have from time to time questioned the institution of monogamy, and suggested that there might be other workable and justifiable kinds of marital life. But the idea of monogamy, difficult as it is to practise, does not easily die. We assume it to be the best kind of arrangement, though our assumption is not always based on very reasonable grounds.

For the Christian, however, monogamy is a "good thing," not for reasons of economy, nor for the social welfare, but chiefly because it is of the divine order of creation. It may be that this is a truth understood only by the eyes and ears of faith. It cannot be made clear to the agnostic, or the atheist. But to the theist monogamy is good because there is found in human love and in the human family a *given-ness*, which is the reason why one man should be united with one woman.

Every person is the child of one father and one mother. He is born of a union of only two persons, who are not just bodies, but bodies and souls. Therefore the existence of the child is irrevocably related to two other existences. The bond, the involvement is indissoluble, and all three know it. Sin and error and ignorance may disrupt the union of these three persons, but the fact and knowledge of this bond is never lost. No matter what a person may do within this parent-child relationship, he can never obliterate its uniqueness, nor forget that such a relationship exists.

Moreover it is a fact, I think, that human love (the love of man for woman) at its earthly best is monogamous. Polygamous desires exist no doubt in all of us, at some time or other. But aside from this, and beyond all the ethical obligation in monogamy we feel or ought to feel, it is true that when we are in love we consider the intrusion of a third person to be an evil. In spite of the earthly desires for change and variety which exist through our human sinfulness, natural love at its best is single-minded. We know when we are genuinely in love partly because when it happens, the last thing we care to do is to share the loved one with somebody else. "Two's a company, three's a crowd," to put it mildly.

The Christian, then, is a person who believes that monogamy is of the divine order of things; and he cannot fail to be seriously disturbed by the present situation in regard to family life, for there are clear and numerous signs that its solidarity is breaking up. It is not necessary to quote figures on divorce to demonstrate this. Such statistics are only a part of the evidence. Every person who is married or who has married friends is aware of the fact that family life today rests upon uncertain and shifting foundations.

It will help us to consider some of the causes of this present situation. I do not pretend that this list is final or definitive, since many of the causes are hidden from us, no doubt, within the complex ferment of the culture of our time.

One underlying cause of the uncertainty of family life is that our society has been rapidly shifting from an agricultural to an urban culture; or, to be more accurate, to a suburban culture. We know that this has produced changes in occupations, living conditions, recreation, and the unity of the family itself. In the more agrarian society of fifty or a hundred years ago the family was interdependent in a manner which now rarely exists. Its members worked together, they played together, they worshipped together. With the shift to urban and suburban life this interdependence has been broken up. With the development of technological skills and industrial production on an unprecedented scale, work has been taken away from the home and its immediate environment. Recreation within the home has not only been shattered by forms of outside sports and spectator activities, but even within the home it is no longer a self-made kind of thing. The modern family does not amuse itself as a family any more. Six separate individuals may have six separate radios, or TV sets, and listen in six different rooms to six different programs.

This is all too obvious to expand. One has only to think of the tremendous rise in our century of clubs, societies, organizations, planned activities for children outside the home, and new means of transportation, to realize the influences which have been brought about by this movement away from the land and into the cities; into a mass-production culture.

Another clear-cut cause for the present precarious situation of the family is the breakdown of religious faith and its by-product the moral law. We live in a time when all institutions have been called into question; all philosophies and religious assumptions have been viewed with a new, bold skepticism. In the intellectual convulsions of the last hundred years, the ancient, simple, childlike faith in God has been lost. We turn to Him in need, and in wistfulness and in hunger, but too few turn to Him with naturalness and without a gnawing doubt. With this loss of the supernatural ground of our life there has been an accompanying loss of faith in the validity of the moral law and of ethical systems—even a loss of faith in man. The family is but one of the institutions which have been rocked and tossed about by these intellectual convulsions. We are living in a time when to many people the old rules simply do not seem to apply.

I presume that a corollary of this loss of faith in religion and morals, and another cause of the present situation, is the escape from Puritanism. Within the overwhelming wave of humanistic thought, Puritanism has fallen by the wayside, and on the whole there is some cause for rejoicing that it has. Men have refused not only to believe in hell but to live

in it. They have rebelled against many taboos, super-
stitions, and temporary conventions which some
years ago masqueraded as divine law and unalterable
truth. They have rebelled (though not sufficiently
in the last postwar years) against Biblical Funda-
mentalism and absolute standards of ethical behavior as set forth by fallible Churches and sects.

Among other things this has had something to do
with the rise of the divorce rate. In a more Puritanical society, man and wife often lived together for
many years in loveless endurance, or in open and
constant warfare, in preference to what was understood as disobedience to the law of God binding
them forever and for aye in any time or place and
under any circumstance. With Puritanism swept
away, men and women are more likely to separate or to seek divorce, since they no longer believe
in the fixed and unalterable laws of Puritanical
Churches, nor do they risk to as great a degree the
disfavor of their non-Puritanical friends. And surely
there are occasions when a divorce is a more moral
solution than for two hostile, unloving people to
continue to battle one another year after weary
year.

But in this escape from Puritanism there is clearly
a tendency to run as far as possible in the opposite

direction, toward the selfish subjectivism of the "I have a right to my own happiness" way of thinking. Frequently the escape from Puritanism results in libertinism and a rejection of all moral sanctions, laws, ancient institutions, and authorities, including God, the Church, and the historic sanctity of the family.

Another cause of the present situation is perhaps the nature of modern economic competition. The facts in this matter are somewhat slippery, as it appears that our society is in the midst of a change at the present moment. But what I have in mind is this: Back on the farm, or in small-town life some years ago, a man usually married before he was out of his teens, and a girl married almost as soon as she was mature enough to bear children. During the first half of the century, with the increasing necessity of more education so that men could earn their living in a highly competitive society, marriage was more frequently delayed. Men and women, ready for marriage at seventeen or eighteen, postponed the relationship in order to procure the education necessary for adequate breadwinning. Society thus added to the burden of sexual chastity before marriage, and it is undoubtedly true that sexual incontinence before marriage causes some of the problems within marriage. I shall return to this question in a later chapter. However, we know that sex is here to stay, and we ought to recognize the responsibility upon society as a whole to make it possible somehow for men and women to marry those they love at, or near, the age when they are ready for mating.

I say the facts here are somewhat slippery because what seemed to be a trend in my youth is evidently changing. Due both to a shift in philosophy and certainly to an era of prosperity, the present trend seems to be toward earlier marriages. Young couples are happily launching out into the deep, with both husband and wife working, and in many cases with the wife working to earn the living while the husband improves his intellect in some institution of good learning.

Another cause of our situation, already touched upon though not explicitly stated, is what we may call the emancipation of women. I do not go as far as Philip Wylie in attributing half the evils of modern life to what he calls Mom-Worship, but it seems not unreasonable that the escape of women from the home and all its ancient backbreaking duties has had something to do with the breakup of the family as a close-knit unit. Mom did get out of the kitchen— except for a few minutes with the can opener and the plastic containers just before a meal. She also got out of the house; and into innumerable societies, organizations, and agencies. Much of this freedom has been good for Mom, and some of it has been good for the home. No family, no member of a family, should live completely within the walls of one house.

Yet we are aware of instances in which the emancipation of women has led to the neglect of husband and children and resulted in a loss of the real, if complex, distinctions in body and soul between man and woman. It is quite possible that Mom's reckless and continual immersion in random pools of human activity both masculine and feminine has been a subconscious device to get away from the cries of the children and the demands of Pop. For some women of this century anything outside the house has been regarded as more fruitful, more exciting, and more beneficial to society than anything inside the house. And there are times when many men would agree with Mr. Wylie that women have been barging around unintelligently messing things up in various civic matters, organizations, and churches, when they should have been at home crooning lullabies to their babies.

I am not learned enough to describe the emotional, psychic, intellectual, and spiritual distinctions between men and women. I believe that these distinctions really exist, and that the matter is an important question of our time with relevance to the stability of the family. A woman is not simply the physical opposite of a man. In the increased understanding of these real distinctions and of the singular qualities and capacities of woman, there will be an increased understanding of woman's place in the world, and of her unique contributions to the family.

Finally, part of the reason for the moral and spiritual disintegration of family life is the wars in which we have been involved. Human beings can stand only so much tension and fear. A war, with all its loneliness, terror, anxiety, and climactic sinfulness, affects the entire population. There were too many war marriages entered into by those living on borrowed time, seeking some measure of earthly happiness in a time of catastrophe. There is in wartime not only the problem of soldiers away from home, bored, lonely, frightened, with little to look forward to except more loneliness, boredom, fear, and the event of death; there is also the problem of wives and sweethearts at home trying to live nobly in anxiety, yet afflicted with the same human desires, lonelinesses, and fears; susceptible to the same temptations to escape from the grimness of reality. Since sex is one of the chief pathways of escape, wartime always brings with it a relaxation of the established ethics and mores of sex behavior.

Also to be considered is the aftermath of war, with its inevitable release from fear, with its "blowing off of steam," which again results in a loosening of the normal allegiance to moral codes and ideals. As one who played in a professional dance orchestra during the "roaring twenties," I could, if pressed, offer a considerable amount of firsthand evidence of this fact. And having travelled about the country from coast to coast for about four years during and following the second World War, I could produce further firsthand evidence of the fact that the emotional tension built up during wars, in soldiers and civilians alike, explodes in many directions with the coming of peace.

These are costs of war. It is not entirely fair to blame these wartime calamities completely upon the individual sinfulness of the flesh. It is the sins of the spirit which produce war, and those sins also are in us all; they are the chief sins—pride, arrogance, covetousness, hatred—and they are more despicable than the sins of the drunken soldier looking for a woman, or the sins of his frustrated, anxious, and lonely wife a thousand or more miles away.

I have attempted to list several of the causes of the breakdown of family life. I suppose actually these causes are mixed together inseparably and to be distinguished only for purposes of investigation and analysis. What we have to remember above all is that we are living in an age of tremendous social, political, and intellectual turmoil. To borrow a phrase from Mr. Hart, the whole world is "bewitched, bothered, and bewildered." I imagine no era in history has witnessed such gigantic changes in so short a time as our own era. The foundations of religion, morality, political institutions, social theory, the very notion of the nature of man—all have been shaken with a great violence. In such a time one must expect violent changes in the life of the family. It would be utterly unrealistic to suppose that in such an age of infection the family could remain uncontaminated.

But Christians have faith that the world is not over, and men's dreams not forever shattered. Christians surely will not "give up" on the family, but will continue to hope for it and to work for its strengthening, that beyond these disastrous times a new and deeper understanding of the foundation and the goal of family life will be found by men.

As when reading a newspaper, we find that the bad in the world crowds out of mind the good, so when considering the family in America, we let the conflicts, separations, unhappinesses which we know about push from our minds the fact that there are exceedingly large numbers of families in which fidelity, trust, and affection grow and deepen within the climate of a godly faith. There are families, many of them, which discover a rich, abiding happiness. These are the most important witnesses to the fact in which the Christian believes: that family life, by the grace of God, is the most normal and most fruitful instrument for the realization of mature manhood, and the most excellent symbol we have on this earth for the Kingdom of God.

Chapter 2

ELEMENTS OF
RECONSTRUCTION

IF WE admit that the present situation of the family is alarming, what can be done to help in the reconstruction of family life?

Much of our discussion about the rehabilitation of family life is highly unrealistic and often irrelevant. It is a weakness of our unredeemed human nature that we always notice first the least important things. Christians, for example, have always been more concerned with the venial, fleshly sins than with the more devastating sins of the spirit. The fleshly sins are more noticeable, of course, and their effect upon the social life is more readily, more immediately discerned. But I often think that our Lord must have suffered intensely through Christian history as Pharisees in the churches have pointed their fingers in scorn and condemnation at drunkards, prostitutes, adulterers, misers, and lazy men. This human obsession with the surface characteristics of life is apparent in many spheres.

I remember a meeting of a ministerial association several years ago, when one of the brethren earnestly desired the association to start a crusade against punchboards, which were in evidence in certain drugstores, restaurants, and other places frequented by teen-agers. Such an idea is not entirely to be condemned if we assume that punchboards are bad for teen-agers. But a punchboard crusade by itself is a little absurd. What would happen? The punchboards would go into the back rooms, where teen-agers could find them without too much difficulty. The slot machines would continue to operate in taverns and country clubs. The big-time gambling among the town's businessmen and fathers of the teen-agers would continue via racing wire, football pool, poker game at the club or private home. It is a little ridiculous to close down the punchboard trade for teen-agers, only to have the teen-ager come home to find Mother losing the grocery money over the bridge table.

The reason people gamble is not that there are punchboards around. It is because they are bored, or possess some inordinate desire for the excitement of risk, or have the wrong conception of the nature of God and of the nature of man's dignity and man's work.

The essential task of churches in a community is not to crusade against punchboards, but to crusade for human souls, and to convert them to a notion of God and man which will make gambling seem rather a waste of time and a threat to the dignity of man and his work. I suppose we shall never overcome entirely our occasional desire to take a chance to get something for nothing. There is a certain mischievous kind of fun in gambling which is of more interest to some people than the loss or acquisition of the money involved. The most pious person would probably want to drop a dollar's worth of quarters in the machines at Harold's Club in Reno, just for the heck of it, without being tempted to stay there all night until his resources were exhausted.

Gambling in its extreme forms is a kind of disease, and it is one more surface evidence of a sick civilization. It is like the pimples on the chin of an adolescent, temporarily sick in spirit; it doesn't do much good to put calamine lotion on the pimples if the trouble is inside.

Sometimes, to take another example, we fall into the same unrealism in regard to our church programs of Christian education. The ignorance of religious matters is colossal. I have taught students in prep school and college and I know how much is unknown by students in general and Episcopal students in particular. Something ought to be done about the illiteracy. We all agree on that. But there is a deeper malady in the Christian soul today which is the root-cause of his illiteracy. He has lost his faith in God. His faith is no longer childlike, natural, instinctive, and spontaneous. Until this faith is restored he will not have much interest in the secondary facts of religious lore.

If there is a tone of unreality about some of our educational procedures it is because we turn to the visible, tangible errors and seem to think that if these are corrected the rest will take care of itself. To put it in exaggerated form, a clergyman says to himself, "Joe Doaks is a poor Churchman. He doesn't know any theology or history. He knows nothing about the Prayer Book. He doesn't know a sacrament from a candlestick; he thinks an epistle is a female apostle; he is a dumbbell about religion. I will therefore institute eight courses so that he can learn about God and the Church. Then he will be an intelligent Christian and a good Churchman."

This is really a further evidence of the widespread idea that man can save himself by education; that knowledge will bring virtue. We have to be continually reminded that knowledge about God is not the same as knowledge of God. The purpose of the Church is not to make a vest-pocket theologian out of every layman; it is to convert people to a lively faith in God and His Christ. Instruction is part of the process.

But the most important questions which need answers in our time concern the primary notions about man and his relationship to the universe. For the middle of the twentieth century the basic problems are not Apostolic Succession, the Real Presence, liturgical reform, the history of the Reformation and the like, but such questions as the relation between faith and reason, the nature of revelation, the nature of belief and knowledge. Twentieth-century man unfortunately has an instinctive distrust of faith, revelation, intuitional knowledge. He lives in a world which has more than played with the idea that God is a gigantic illusion. He is not yet ready to grant the possibility that man can know anything except by reason and the "scientific method." He is not at all sure that God has revealed, or will reveal, or can reveal Himself to finite minds.

So we often miss the mark in our educational procedures. We try to get people interested in Church, worship, Christian ethics, who are not sure there is a reason for Church, or any value in worship, or any sanction for ethics beyond human reason and expediency. The first necessity is the rediscovery of God and how He acts upon our world.

The real problem is not to make seminarians out of Sunday school children, but to initiate them into an awareness of the meaning of God within their own daily experience. Information about God and the Church are no substitute for the experience of His presence.

Perhaps this all seems like an unnecessary digression. The point is that, as we often deal with surface sicknesses instead of the deep-seated ailment in our approach to social affairs and education and other matters, so also do we often deal with the surface aspects of marriage and the family—the punch-board aspects. We set about trying to rehabilitate family life by tinkering with surface disorders. Let me illustrate with a highly imaginary example, distorted for reasons of emphasis.

Suppose a family by the name of Guggenheimer. Molly and Thaddeus marry after a year's engagement and settle down to domestic bliss, after a gala wedding and a romantic honeymoon. In due time they are blessed with children: Patrick and Gloria. Thaddeus works hard for ten years, and by that time has a suburban bungalow, two cars, a television set, and twenty thousand dollars worth of life insurance. He appears to be all set, but he is unhappy and doesn't know why. He has spent so much time working that he doesn't know his children and hardly knows his wife.

Molly in the meantime has become interested in movies, bridge, and the daughters of the "Let's Reform the Whole Damn Community" Club, and on the basis of her movie life, her powers of analysis obtained at the bridge table, and her club work, she has started to reform the whole damn community, beginning with Thaddeus. She was a vision to behold on her wedding day, and she still stuccos her façade for the bridge club; but at home she lets herself go and masquerades as a middle-aged squaw from the Andes. On the foundation of a course in child psychology picked up years before at Columbia Teachers College (where they were very slow to become acquainted with the facts of life), she has brought up Patrick progressively, so that by the time he is eight he is a monster right out of Charles Addams' drawings, and Public Enemy Number One for a radius of seventeen blocks in Suburbia. By the time he was five both Mom and Pop could see something was wrong about the course Mom took; so Pop, who once heard a lecture by an old-fashioned educator at a commencement reunion, has put his knowledge to work on Gloria. At the age of six she has turned into a scared, jumpy little seedling doomed to no bloom.

At this juncture Thaddeus has begun to take a couple of cocktails in the Biltmore Bar before catching the 5:17. He has to take away the nervous jitters acquired making money. Before dinner he has two more drinks, so he can walk through the littered house without tripping, and to ease the impact of the reform movement which his "Little Sweetie" begins as soon as he gets into the house.

He shares his Manhattans with Molly, who with two under her broadening girdle becomes a first-class substitute for a communist commissar confronted with three capitalists. Molly has played bridge all afternoon, so the dinner comes out of Heinz's hottest cans and Birdseye's coldest lockers. After this feast the worm turns and blasts the little Missus back into the kitchen, while the junior Monster is hacking the piano to pieces with a car-jack and Gloria is having a tantrum in the bathroom.

At this crossroads in the journey through marital bliss, Thaddeus happens to hire a new secretary in the office. She is not out to reform anything, except the ideas of social behavior her fundamentalist father tried to palm off on her, and she has not only pretty eyes but also a touch of Venus from the neck down. One thing leads to another, and pretty soon Thaddeus is off to the races and glad to get away from home.

Molly cries on the shoulder of her pastor, who hasn't seen her or Thaddeus in church for three years, and the pastor tells her to come back to church, offers a prayer, and counsels her on Christian patience and sacrifice. What else can he do? Molly gets a book out of the library, the first book she has seen for months, gives up movies, and tries to straighten things out by taking hip-exercises and making Floating Island for dessert three nights in succession. She reads that it is a good thing for families to play together, so she tries to get Thaddeus, Gloria, and the Monster out into the back yard for croquet, as a postwar project in reconstruction. Thaddeus has got the gate from the secretary, and he is in a stew; half-penitent, but still unwilling to reform himself from everything he thinks makes him distinctive. The croquet game, as a kind of beneficial therapy, doesn't even get through the first wicket. Finally Molly goes to see the secretary of the "You Too Can Have a Happy Family" Society, who suggests a ten-week course in folk dancing as an instrument of transfiguration.

Now, in spite of this ridiculous distortion, there are families like this. You know some of them. Not one of the characters is fundamentally mean, cruel, vicious, unloving. Not one is intentionally trying to shatter his family life. The most vicious one is the little Monster and you can't blame his depravity on him alone.

The fact is that when a family gets into such a state of boredom, crotchetiness, disorder, and insensitivity, the Church and the Better Families bureaus come along with superficial remedies. Go back to church, says the parson. Take up folk dancing and psychoanalysis, says the secular expert. Read more good books, be more patient, think positively, and while we don't believe in prayer, you might go to church as a project in doing things together. This is cold turkey to Thaddeus and Molly. They have been doing too many things together already. So they may sweat it out for fifty years, or they may get divorced.

The real problem is both complex and simple— simple to discern and complex to solve. It is a difficulty not to be cured by folk dancing or even going to church together. Such a family reveals the wrong conception of the nature of man, his dignity and worth. Such a family reveals the wrong idea of the reality and nature of God, of the meaning of worship, faith, duty, responsibility, and love. They expected both too much and too little. Perhaps they had the wrong idea of sex to begin with and tried to think it was of no particular importance in comparison with their spiritual love for each other, or (which is more likely in this age) they thought sexual love was the only important thing and that they could live on that alone.

So there has been a great disillusionment and a disaster. No talks on the evils of drinking and adultery, no platitudes on the value of going to church or playing ping-pong together will redeem the disaster.

If there was some germ of true love and good companionship in the first place, a redemption may take place. What is needed is not instruction but conversion—an almost complete transformation of the personalities involved. If there was no real love even at the beginning of the marriage, even a conversion of the individuals will probably not help. What we are dealing with in so many cases is the same thing Arthur Miller dealt with in *Death of a Salesman*—a person or persons who have all the wrong ideas about everything that is important: God, man, the nature of marriage, the meaning of human existence.

I am not opposed to marriage counsellors, visits to the pastor, booklets on how to stop drinking, how to stop flirting with other women, or how to save your family life. I believe more attention should be directed to the roots of the problem. The contemporary situation of family life demands that the whole matter be treated with thoughtfulness and seriousness. There is no easy way to have a happy marriage. There is no ten-week course in counselling which can redeem a wrecked marriage.

The reconstruction of family life is a difficult task. It involves first of all the recovery of faith in God and the by-product of that faith, a recognition of man's profoundly complex and otherworldly nature. It involves the faith that man's nature cannot realize itself truly without relationship to God and the immersion of all natural love in His love. It involves a fact we have too easily forgotten. Love is not something you have at the beginning of marriage and then lose. Love is something to be won, through the losing of life in all the years of marriage, in every difficulty and tribulation, in every delight and joy. When man and wife work together through the years to achieve fidelity, understanding, companionship, and romance too, in spite of sickness, poverty, loss, or tragedy, the love which emerges at the end of life is much more "a many-splendor'd thing" than the romantic and unknowing love at the beginning, which was in fact simply a yearning and a faith that love could grow.

The disease that infects the modern family is rooted in the superficial humanistic ideas of nature, and of man and God, which have been the cause of infection in our whole culture. These same ideas have made a shambles of American education, deluded us into thinking that love is something out of a Class B picture from Hollywood, and made us believe that man can achieve all things through will power, right reason, and sexual adjustment.

If we are realistic we must admit that the failure within many families is too complete to do anything about except to be compassionate, charitable, and just. But our task, again, is not to sit wringing our hands and crying, "See what's happened to family life." It is the task of turning to those who are not yet immersed in disaster, and of trying to help in the establishment of stronger foundations.

The first foundation, I think, is to help modern men and women, especially the younger ones, to recover their faith in a living God of love who acts upon the human spirit, and by whose grace all human affections can be deepened and made meaningful and all human calamities surmounted.

Chapter 3

THE RECOVERY OF FAITH

A GREAT many people have told us that there is a religious revival going on in America today, and statistically this seems to be a fact. More people are joining churches. More people are attending churches. I think anyone who has followed the ups and downs of American religious life over the past twenty years is aware that there is indeed an increased interest in Christianity, a desire to know more about it, and if possible to do something about it.

But the revival is only skin deep, and it is often confused with patriotism. It has not only become rather popular to be a member of a Church; it is something every good American does. There is no indication yet that the revival has reached the area of public and private morality. The students in my community are relatively active in their church attendance. Their batting average, so to speak, is if anything better than that of our adult members. But their religious convictions have not yet made any noticeable difference in their weekend behavior.

The southern section of the country is a veritable seedbed of religious revivals. The tents of the evangelists mushroom all over the landscape. But the southern section of the country, in spite of its churchgoing and its revivals, is not ready to deal with the number one social problem of the nation: segregation.

Actually we are confronted in all parts of the country with a curious situation. I imagine there are more people who believe in the Church than there are people who believe in God. Undoubtedly most people think they believe in the existence of some kind of God. But I mean belief in the Christian God; belief in a God in whose goodness we can trust, on whose forgiveness we can count, to whom we can continually and fruitfully make our prayer.

There are very many churches and some of them seem to be thriving, but the primary rock on which they stand has crumbled considerably. In spite of the increase of Church membership it is difficult to distinguish the "pillar of the Church" from the "pillar of the country club." They both think about the same way.

It ought never to be surprising that Christians, among others, should fail to live according to the principles of Christ. Such failure is everlasting, and it is to be understood by a realist as the inevitable condition of sinful and ignorant human beings. What *is* surprising is that so many people, even Church people, fail to see that to believe in God really means to trust in His goodness and His sovereignty over the earth. A Christian ought, in spite of his failure, to turn to God as naturally as a flower turns toward the sun. But even at Church meetings, after an opening prayer and a religious discussion, Christians often give no evidence that they believe God is anywhere around. Their real trust is elsewhere; generally in a spurious humanism which looks to man for the solution of human problems. The deep root of religion has been pulled out, and unless it is put back soon into a more fertile earth the tree cannot last long.

If there is any truth in this diagnosis, we must set about the rediscovery of God. And, paradoxically, I believe we must first turn our attention upon man. This looks, I know, like a suggestion that we return to the humanism which has been our near-downfall. But I hope I can make clear that I am speaking of another kind of humanism which can lead us from this world to the Being of God. It is because of the unusual temper of the mind of modern man with all its curious and twentieth-century assumptions and presuppositions that I think we cannot start with God and come down. Man is where we have to begin.

This is an age when the confusion in thought and morals has been so great that in order to regain our footing we have to go back before theology, to investigate honestly the nature of man, in order to see what facts about him give reasonable evidence that he possesses qualities and characteristics which point beyond him himself; so that the only truly reasonable explanation of him is one that is supernatural.

Anthropomorphism cannot be avoided. There is no place to begin except with man. All that we know about the world, ourselves, and God we know through man. Let us be humanists to this extent: that we shall begin where we have to begin, on earth instead of in heaven, and work upward, as it were, to see if man in the full complexity of his nature can be explained without assuming the existence of a creative and redemptive God. The tentative acceptance of God as a reasonable source and ground of man's being is no substitute for the knowledge of the living God possessed by men of faith and devotion. But there is not much chance that men will come into this personal knowledge unless they are able to understand that it is not really possible to account for human being without assuming Divine Being.

It may be a fact that a man cannot be argued into religion. But reasonable men can be persuaded to move outward toward more inclusive truth. Perhaps in the time of Christ the procedure I am speaking about would have had little meaning. In that time a universe without a creative, just, and merciful God would have been an unreasonable assumption. Today it is the idea of a universe with such a God which is widely questioned and even more widely disregarded.

In the approach to this matter, then, we have to begin again with people (especially with those young in years), to speak in terms relevant to their experience, and without a theological jargon. For it is important to convert them to the knowledge that religion is not something apart from life but something made of the stuff of life itself; and that God is not a Being known only to a few mystical people, but a Being known in some way to every man, though every man may not know His name, nor understand the fullness of His revelation.

Religious experience is common to all men. Alan Richardson has this to say:

It may well be that we do not know that we know God, but it cannot be true that we do not in fact know Him. Whenever we are moved to search for truth or are prompted to do a generous action; whenever we burn with indignation at injustice or shudder at something which is ugly; whenever we feel joy in a beautiful work of nature or of art, we are in reality subject to the pressure of God's presence upon our lives, and we should learn to recognize in all such things the beginnings of our knowledge of God.[1]

This general, common experience known to all men is a direct, concrete, vivid awareness of the world and its meaning. It is to be distinguished from the theology, Christian or otherwise, which is the by-product of religious experience. This is to say that the doctrines of a Church are no substitute for, nor are they equal to, the religious experience. They help us to make rational, articulate, and systematic the vivid, unsystematic, rich, and somewhat irrational moments which make up the experience itself. Theology therefore is primarily a matter for the expert, the clergyman, the trained layman, the philosopher. It is a shorthand language, so to speak, signifying to the informed the rich and unutterable experience. The layman, particularly the layman

[1] Alan Richardson, *The Gospel and Modern Thought* (London: Oxford University Press, 1950).

of today, is not so concerned with this abstract of religion as he is with the experience itself. The unbeliever may be "bewitched, bothered, and bewildered" by life. He is an ignoramus about theology. But being human he has enough perception to know that the heart of religion is not in theology. He knows that if God does exist He must be apprehended through the motley, multicolored pattern of human existence and revealed through man's daily experience. He has not been able to find God with any assurance through this pattern and experience, and in many cases it is because we have not made it clear to him what kind of God we are talking about, in words and ideas which are consistent and relevant to his experience.

An English clergyman once said: "People have no time for religion; they have time only for faith." People have work to do in the world, and not much time for the interesting but secondary matters of theological speculation. A layman does not have to understand the history and theology of the Nicene Creed in order to be a good Christian, any more than a man has to be a lawyer in order to be a good citizen, or a person has to know harmony and counterpoint to appreciate good music. Such intellectual understanding certainly increases a man's knowledge but not necessarily his faith. The goal of the Church is to help people to live a Christian life, to have some continuing and personal experience of God, to be spiritually whole.

So it appears to me that the great need of this time is to help men to recover faith in a few basic dogmas: that God exists as sovereign of all creation, in whom man can trust and hope; that Jesus is the climactic expression in human life of the character of God; that man by himself cannot save himself, because he is finite and a sinner. There are no doubt a few others. However, the tendency to want to stuff ecclesiastical formulas down the throat of every Christian from kindergarten to the Old Folks' Home is not in itself going to accomplish much, except to turn out breathing encyclopedias of Church lore. What we are after is to rediscover for man the fact that the experiences which gave rise to theological speculation can be recaptured in this generation according to the knowledge, perception, and imagination of people today.

I do not by any means wish to imply that theology is not important, for it is of the utmost importance. I do not even mean that laymen should never have to learn the meaning of technical terms. But I do think they must first learn again that the technical term is valid only if there is a concrete and meaningful experience for which it is a symbol. The technical term will never mean anything to them until they have had the experience existentially, to use the popular phrase.

We have been talking about the Real Presence to people who have no idea of Eucharist or communion or sacrifice. We have been speaking of Holy Communion to those who have no understanding of a sacramental universe, and of a sacramental universe to those who have no idea of the nature of God, and of the nature of God to those who are not even sure He exists. We have, in the matter of marriage, been speaking of the sanctity of the individual, of responsibility and duty and sacrifice, to people who in many cases believe that man is only a rather extraordinarily complex rat.

The technical terms cannot of course be entirely avoided. But when they are used they ought surely to be explained and understood with reference to the vivid and concrete and factual everyday life of living persons. It is not a definition of salvation, either by Calvin or Aquinas, that man needs to know. What he needs to know is whether Christ can save him from the sins and evils, fears and anxieties, that he knows daily in his twentieth-century life; and if so, how does this salvation work, how can it be achieved, and to what quality of life does it lead?

If it is true that marriage cannot achieve its real meaning and possible richness without God, then all men must know this; but they will not come to understand it well until they recover something of their knowledge of man, of the fact that he is Adam a sinner, and Job a sufferer, strung between two worlds, heaven and earth. In this earthly pilgrimage he is pain-blasted, grief-burnt, reason-taunted, yet without rational explanation for love, guilt, fear, suffering, birth, death.

In this life there is a sadness in man's heart as indigenous to the earth as stone, and a restlessness not fulfilled even in the happiest family. Man has to learn again, and help others to learn, that he is a failure at everything. In the midst of this earthly journey it is to be hoped that some time or other there will come to every man as he stands in the grip of pain and sin and fear a glimpse of the Cross, rising out of the vortex of meaninglessness above the earth itself—the condemnation of all pride and notion of godliness; the sign that until a man is ready to die to life, life is not given.

In the sight of this Cross a man may see for the

first time the world in a new perspective, its very shape transformed, as love crosses out the insufferable marks of crucifixion. This has something to do with family life. For until there is such a recovery of faith in God's forgiveness and love, caught and held within the knowledge of the tragedy of earthly life, there can never be a truly growing, sharing, understanding family.

Until men and women recover this cliff-edged faith, so that they can look with hope to the future, and beyond the future to eternal life, they will always be earthbound, worldly in their desires and selfish in their aspirations and with an insufficient knowledge of their own human natures to accomplish their real purpose as parents and lovers; without the strength to overcome "every root of bitterness, the desire for vainglory and the pride of life."

Chapter 4

LOVE AND SEX

SEVERAL years ago I took my small daughter for an automobile ride to visit her grandparents. It was one of those days at the end of summer when the world stands still for a golden moment before rushing off into the red and brown of autumn. My daughter asked the customary questions of childhood as we drove along: "What's that and why? How soon and when? How long before we get there?" And then after a long pause she said, "I'd like to go to the end of the world. I bet it's an awful long way."

"What for?" I asked.

"To see what it's like," she answered.

She expressed something common to all men, the abiding quest of the spirit. I wanted to say, "You will go to the end of the world, my child, as all men go to the end of the world. There will be other halcyon days like this when the whole earth is dressed in gold, and beauty dances on every summer hill. There will be days without sun, and the road will wind down into the valleys under the godless stars. It may be a long journey, it may be short. You'll need a map for the journey, and a lantern for the dark, and some good companions. I hope you find them. I hope there will be in you at the end of life as there is at the beginning this bright, glad search for loveliness and for adventure, and for truth; like the sound of a bugle on a cloudless morning."

All men look for something. They want to go to the end of the world, to know the fullness of the earth. They are filled with desires, urgent and sometimes contradictory. They search for a lost river, a magic key to a forgotten garden that is filled with meaning.

Men want food, shelter, and a measure of security. They want freedom and a place on the land; a feeling of belonging to the earth. They want a mate; at least one other person with whom in the nakedness of the spirit and the flesh they can search out the depths of human love. All of us have these thirsts; all of us desire to make the journey to the end of the world, knowing something of pain, loneliness, laughter, beauty, and the shining of truth. We search for meaning and for hope. And all this is concrete evidence recognized by reasonable men which casts a light upon our natures, and reveals us to be creatures tensed between two worlds; torn between earth and some otherworldly heaven.

In the desire of man for a mate, and in his experience of sexual love, as well as in his other desires, is the evidence that man is destined not for the earth alone. The sexual love of man for woman is of the divine order of creation, and it is difficult to explain man's knowledge and experience of it without reference to the mark of divinity within him.

The majority of people find, if anywhere, the fullness of earthly life with some person of the opposite sex. We take this given attraction to be normal. It is not a minor matter in life, nor is love purely spiritual. The normal human being was made to love somebody not only with the spirit but in the flesh.

There are, it is true, those persons who for one reason or another never find anybody to love, or whose love is not reciprocated in equal fashion, or who through the sinfulness and ignorance of mankind seem only to love, as we say, unnaturally. About these people we can only say, "All things are possible with God."

The unmarried person, man or woman, who has never found someone to be loved by, or to love, can surely find some fullness of life through some commitment to God or humankind. Yet the person who is a bachelor or spinster involuntarily must frequently know a certain emptiness, and this must have its own peculiar sadness for which there is no apparent compensation, except the knowledge that married people, too, have their own peculiar sadness.

Of those who are bachelors and spinsters by choice, or by vocation, I suppose you'd say, "They have their reward." They are unencumbered, free of the responsibilities and difficulties of marriage. For them the freedom, or the sense of vocation, may make up for the family happiness they miss.

Of those who find erotic love with persons of their own sex we can say only that the sin is usually not theirs alone. They are to be treated with understanding and intelligence, as we treat other people who are sick. There are matters here which surpass our understanding too much to allow us to condemn outright such variations in behavior from the normal.

But most of us find the most consuming love of which we are capable with some member of the opposite sex. That's as obvious as grass.

I suppose to write about sex in a book about religion is always a little exciting, as it is to read about it. Church people always titter a little uncomfortably when the subject is mentioned from the pulpit or in a conference. We have not escaped sufficiently from Puritanism, which considered sex a somewhat unclean garment of the spirit. There is also a certain modesty and restraint which ought to mark any civilized and Christian discussion of a matter so personal and so close to the sacred and unsearchable springs of life. There are people today who, having escaped from Puritanism, would advocate unrestrained discussions of sex in all its manifestations, so that nothing should be held back. Sex education, according to these persons, ought to be similar to the education of a butcher. One should go at the problem of sex with an open admission of the fact that man is nothing but a promiscuous rabbit with shrunken ears who walks upright. I do not hold to this viewpoint.

The first thing I'd like to say about sex begins with a quotation from the Old Testament: "Speak to the earth, and it shall teach thee" (Job 12:8).

The earth can teach us a great deal, and one of the things it can teach is naturalness. We are an over-mannered, over-urbanized society. We drink tea with a little finger pointing out into the air; we play golf like helicopters taking off with the morning mail; instead of saying simply, "He died," we say, "He passed away."

Among the unnatural attitudes of many moderns is our attitude toward sex. America has a curious obsession with the subject. We do not talk very much about it in polite society, or even in the bosom of the family. But in movie, TV, radio, magazine, novel, advertising, and Pullman car the same old theme shrieks at us. There is not much vitality about it. The obsession is sly, furtive, somewhat slimy. We act like old men with all passion spent, tittering over the imaginary escapades of youth.

Something is wrong with our society in this respect. Boston often bans the most moral plays and books of the year, as though that center of antique culture could not face the natural nudity of the earth. What Boston condemns the rest of the nation reads with furtive giggles. Our newsstands are crowded with sexy stories and pictures, devoid of wonder, naturalness, and vigor; composed perhaps by frigid women and impotent men who have not sufficient earthly vitality to get through the day without a jar of vitamins and a box of tranquillizing pills.

"Speak to the earth, and it shall teach thee." The morality of the back yard is worse than the morality of the barnyard. Behind our prim exterior, all kinds of perversions and exploitations are carried on. Men in the prime of manhood make up for their sex frustrations by telling nasty jokes; and women behind an artificial façade of glamour play at being daring and seductive, half frightened that somebody will take them seriously. Anything natural is better than something unnatural. And nothing supernatural can enter man's spirit, cleansing and purifying his natural passions, until he first recognizes the goodness of the earth, and admits honestly to himself that he is of the earth earthy.

In back of this corporate hypocrisy we are a sexy people. As much so, I suppose, as any other people. We pretend to be a chaste and monogamous nation. We pretend our women's clothes are designed to be attractive to other women. We pretend the movies and TV comedians and newsstands do not really represent our interests. But we are not as lily-pure as we like to pretend. I do not have to prove this with statistics that you can find anywhere. We know it to be a fact. What is annoying and harmful is that our pretension involves us in all kinds of absurd, hypocritical, and unrealistic hanky-panky. We pretend, for instance, that if we get a bunch of soldiers together in a USO canteen and feed them cocoa and crackers in between ping-pong games, they will then abandon all desire (as somebody has said) to "take Betty into the shrubs."

It would do us good to read again W. H. Hudson's *Green Mansions*; to boycott the movies, or most of them, for the rest of the year, with their dreary innuendos of people unmussed and unnatural, panting in a pseudo-passion. It might be well to form a vigilante committee to tear down all the mean, cheap, furtive, and suggestive billboards and to replace them with nudes by Rubens, Rembrandt, Botticelli, and others who looked with a more precise and less lustful eye upon the fact of human flesh. Recall the words: "There be three things which are too wonderful for me, yea, four which I know not: The way of an eagle in the air; the way of a serpent upon a rock; the way of a ship in the midst of the sea; and the way of a man with a maid" (Proverbs 30:18-19).

It is the wonder of it which we have lost. And it is the wonder of it which is one of the strongest evidences we have that man is not simply of the earth. For it seems profoundly true that this natural and earthy experience, which man shares with the animal kingdom, can be an experience through which man is most aware of something supernatural; of a spirituality which possesses him and his loved one, uniting them in a holiness of beauty which is beyond good and evil, and brings them to an understanding of a love which strikes deep to the heart of life's meaning.

And the curious, indeed the terrible thing about sex is that the act which between lovers can be a sacred and holy experience, the same act participated in without love has about it an aura of animality, almost of subhumanness.

To be sure, there seem to be many persons who can enjoy sex without love, and who suffer no particular feelings of guilt, or of falling from a high estate, by such experiences. But their experiences fall short of full humanness. Perhaps some of these people are incapable of love; perhaps more of them have never known the distinction between lusting sexuality and sexual love. It would seem true that those who have experienced sex within the bond of love know it is "too wonderful" to be desecrated or adulterated through alliances without this love.

Now, while we recognize what *ought* to be in the matter of sex, so great and dominating is the sex impulse that we are all adulterers in a spiritual, if not a legalistic, sense. And we know the problem of sex in society is the problem of overcoming concupiscence in fact as well as in fancy. To follow the dictates of the sexual impulse, without restraint, even when we think we are in love, would doom the individual and society to a state of considerable if not complete degeneration. Certainly we are correct in our attempts to curb the practice of fornication and adultery. Sex between lovers can be a holy thing, even, I suspect, between puppy-lovers. But society is correct, and so is religion, in making attempts to regularize the sexual life of the people. Society has to do this for its protection. Religion does it because it understands that love is most holy, and the sexual expression of it most meaningful, when those involved have committed themselves to each other and accepted the full responsibilities of a permanent, lifelong contract; to live together "for better for worse, for richer for poorer, in sickness and in health."

It is, I believe, true that sex between lovers can be evidence of the fact that man is not simply of the earth earthy. But one of the gigantic difficulties for many individuals in this life is to decide what love is, and to limit his expression of a "love" which often seems to be very inclusive. I have an idea that most men and women really desire one mate, some children, one home, and the responsibilities of fidelity and sacrifice that go with this ideal. But there are evils, both in society and in men, which threaten and often contradict and nullify this dream. I am told that some anthropologists believe man is by nature polygamous; and others believe that man is monogamous in essential desire, but polygamous because of ignorance, or sinfulness, or force of circumstances. However this may be, we know that the sexual impulse is one of considerable power, and that it is easy for most of us to confuse true love with sexual attraction.

The normal young person falls in love many times, perhaps, before he finds his "true love." Sometimes he never seems sure which one the "true love" is. For a young man of twenty, it is easy to fall desperately in love with the Queen of the Apple Festival, or the Princess of the Ice Carnival. It is probably true that even on the basis of this romantic infatuation the sexual expression of such love might be quite devoid of sheer lust, and approach some wholeness of meaning. This kind of infatuation and romantic love might conceivably happen a half dozen times—to the confusion of the young Romeo who would suddenly find himself confronted with the fact that he has had a love of some kind or other for six different queens, all of whom were perfectly delightful.

In this dilemma in which our society and our young people often find themselves, it is necessary to turn back to a point I stated earlier. The romantic love with which two young people begin marriage is hardly love at all. It is simply enough trust in one another, and attraction to one another, to enable them to say, "We will take the risk, believing our love will grow into something lasting and ultimately real."

For the fact is (as a student said to me), a man, living in a city of seventy thousand, could undoubtedly find twenty girls within the city with whom he could fall in love and live a happy and constructive life. Our romantic movies and books have led us astray with their implication that there is only one girl in the world for every boy, and that unless he happens to find that one he will lead a dog's life. True love is not something that happens at the beginning of courtship. At that stage it is difficult to distinguish it from the healthy sexual desire of man for woman and woman for man. True love is something you may have after you've been married for ten, twenty, or fifty years. The student was correct, I think. The problem does not involve travelling all over the world to find the one Jill who was meant for a particular Jack. The problem is to find a mate, a person toward whom one feels romantically inclined, and with whom one discovers he is at least fairly congenial, and scarcely ever bored; and then to marry her, to discover by the grace of God and infinite patience how much sex can mean as love grows within the bond of marriage, with all the responsibilities that marriage involves.

It is therefore proper that both the Church and society should continue to hold up the ideal of monogamy and to curb the random sexual adventures of the people. The ideal in Hebrew-Christian ethics is to be strenuously upheld. Chastity before marriage is a great good to be desired, for the sexual experience, so intimate, so profound, so complicated in the spiritual and emotional structure of man, involves the giving of the whole person, which cannot be done without love, and which ought not to be done outside of the binding loyalty of lifelong marriage, for the guilt, or sorrow, or loneliness it may cause.

Yet having presented the ideal, it is proper also to remember that we are but flesh, and weakly human. The sexual impulse is of such considerable power in our lives that from adolescence on it is of major importance to every person; and its control is difficult. If it is denied its legitimate expression within marriage, it is most likely to express itself in some other way, naturally or unnaturally.

A glance at the history of man is sufficient to show that only a rare handful of saints have been able to sublimate sex so completely that its restraints will cause no noticeable detriment to the personality.

It is because we sometimes refuse to face these facts of our sexual nature that Church people often talk nonsense when speaking of sex. In our society at present—with birth control methods known to every high school student, with the danger of venereal disease lessened by a proper knowledge, with hell taken out of popular religion and heaven a remote possibility, and with the moral law pretty well shaken up—in such a society as this the male college student who has not had some sort of sex experience by the time of graduation is perhaps the rare exception.

I went to a summer conference a few years ago and listened while an admirable and idealistic parson gave a talk to college students on the subject of courtship, which in his interpretation ought not to include any sexual expression even of the mildest form until marriage. This is surely a lofty ideal, but it seems to make little sense within the culture of our time. The students asked a few polite questions. That night we had folk dancing and singing to keep their minds on wholesome activities. After that we had a campfire. After that the counsellors went around flushing twenty different couples out of the bushes. With or without lecture they had paired off, as young people will, to engage in various adolescent and, in this case, relatively mild forms of "love-making."

I do not know any complete answer to this prevalent problem. But let's be honest about it. This sort of thing has gone on for many years, and talks about chastity are not going to stop it, unless we can present chastity as a more positive and more profoundly meaningful virtue than we have done for many years. If we are willing to go back before birth control and hand out no more "sex education"; if we are willing to put hell-fire back into religion and let venereal disease go its ravaging way; if we are willing to bring up our children with a fear and distaste for sexual love, we might—perhaps —cut down on the sexual experimentations of adolescence. Even all that would not obliterate it. There were plenty of illegitimate children born in the days when people considered sex an odious custom, and when hell was a fiery furnace.

Somehow we have to convince young people that fornication is a bad preparation for marriage. I am sure millions of married lovers wish that they had remained chaste until their marriage with the one person they loved above all others on earth. But I rather doubt that every form of sexual expression is a bad preparation for marriage. There can be an elementary awkwardness about a kiss, or even holding hands, which may well be eliminated before marriage.

It ought to be a part of our Christian thought on the subject to recognize that the shy, experimental, wondering gropings of adolescence spring from the search for life and meaning. They are not to be construed as simply the animalistic desires of thoroughly bestial creatures. If this desire, seeking one of the deepest experiences man can know, should go beyond the traditions, laws, and customs of society, and the youthfully sincere intentions of a full-blooded person, we should at least not be surprised nor vindictive. Let him that is without sin cast the first stone.

Among other adult pretensions it may be that we pretend this adolescent appearance of promiscuity, or even the fact of it, is worse than it really is. I mean worse morally. It is indeed possible that many who read this book will remember not only past indiscretions, but experiences of which they are ashamed. Yet most of them will recognize, I imagine, that there are more ruinous sins than fornication, and that there are sins within marriage more devastating to the security of marriage than adultery, devastating as that is. God forbid that we should pretend to have been perfectly innocent in our youth, as we cluck our tongues concerning young love at good old Siwash College.

The Christian, standing within the long Hebrew-Christian tradition, and before the fact of the power and mystery of sex, need not be speechless. He can, in fact he must, uphold the ideal and state what he knows to be true: that sexual love is too holy, too wonderful a thing between two lovers to be desecrated and cheapened. He upholds the ideal that this union should ideally take place between those who have accepted the lifelong responsibilities of marriage. He upholds chastity before marriage as a positive and meaningful virtue.

Yet knowing the immense power of the desire for meaning and the sexual drives of man he will never be particularly surprised when men fall from these ideals. At that point he will offer the forgiveness of Christ through the Church to those who sin in this matter as in others.

There can be little doubt that for morally sane people the sins of the flesh bring to men and women what is often a crippling guilt, and a self-loathing which itself can be a continuing detriment to the happiness of marriage. In answer to this the Church announces the freedom and joy of God's forgiveness; and the penitent may discover either in his general or private confession, or through the sacramental confession to God through His appointed priests, that release from guilt and remorse which only God can give; a liberation which enables man to go on with confidence within the bonds of marriage, unrestricted and unfettered by the forgiven sins of the past.

Yet every Christian to be realistic must remember that sex was here before the Church, before the Puritans, before the Ten Commandments. Right from the Garden of Eden. We are not going to change this characteristic of man's nature to find a mate and to know the wonder of man's way with a maiden. The laws, the economy, the customs, even the religion will have to change before this impulse is changed or controlled according to the idealistic notions that some men hold.

I would like to close this chapter by repeating one idea. Within marriage, the sexual experience is a natural, not an ecclesiastical, sacrament. It belongs to the order of creation. It is to be enjoyed. If it is not enjoyed something is wrong with the marriage. One thing for Christians to discover in marriage is that sex is possibly the most spiritual experience of marriage as well as the most earthy. In the union of body and soul, within the knowledge of a mutually self-sacrificing love, there is a wonder and an awareness of the dignity of man lifted from nature to super-nature, in a given experience of love that is both human and divine.

If Christians, believers in the Incarnation, cannot find within marriage the fullness of this sexual experience, and find it with a reckless, clean, wholesome, uninhibited abandon, then we have somehow failed to understand the nature of man, the nature of our religion, the nature of our God, who sanctified and blessed by His presence this fleshly life; and the marriage stands in jeopardy from this lack of understanding.

Chapter 5

THE CHILDREN

SPEAKING objectively, the primary purpose of marriage is procreation; the preservation of the species. Subjectively it is true that most people marry, not because they are zealously concerned to preserve the human race, but because they are attracted to each other and wish to plumb the depths of human love. The sexual experience of man and wife is a legitimate experience whether or not there are children.

But I feel sure that a Christian believes the fullness of marriage can be realized only within a family of children, even though some or all of them may have to be adopted.

No matter how romantically a couple may be in love, and how devoted to one another, there is a slackening of romantic love at least in the physical sense as the years pass; and no doubt one of the difficult times of marriage is that time when the early ardor begins to cool, and man and woman find there must be something in their relationship beyond romantic love, if that relationship is to be kept enduring and strong.

Children, even if they had no other purpose, help in the stabilization of the home, in the growth of affection and patience and devotion within marriage. But quite clearly children are not brought into the world simply to cement the ties of parents. The cosmic purpose and end of marriage is the rearing of children, and caring for them until they are grown up and ready to leave the family nest.

Many people seem to have forgotten this. Both men and women often act as though their sole purpose were to seek their own pleasures and desires. One often hears a mother saying: "What have I got to look forward to? Years of drudgery; the same old thing day after day." One often sees fathers who are sick of their work and feel caught in an endless round of toil; as though life had robbed them of their just deserts.

They have expected too much of this world. For it is man's purpose to live and love and enjoy the earth for a season, without giving his heart to it completely; and to raise children and care for them that life may go on. People too frequently act as if parenthood were a burden, and feel that they have missed their destiny if they do not accomplish big things in the world. They dream dreams too glamorous of what the earth ought to give, and what the world ought to do for them, and they neglect in one fashion or another the children that they have brought into the world.

In the task of trying to build a Christian home, the first thing to remember, I think, is that we have in our hands the destiny of a certain number of individuals. A family is a unit; but it is a unit made up of separate and distinct individuals. This in itself requires some adventure in patience and understanding.

No doubt psychology has done much to help us raise children with wisdom. Yet I cannot but feel that there are certain dangers to which parents have become exposed because of the increased and amateurish knowledge of "psychology."

One danger is that having too little knowledge we tend to minimize individuality. Mama reads a book that says most six-year-old children are shy, or bold, or whatever they are, in general, supposed to be. Mama then assumes that all six-year-olds ought to be shy and worries herself sick if little Johnny at the age of six is as brash as a Ford salesman.

Papa reads a book which says that children of ten ought to learn to play with others, and that they do not like to be by themselves, if they are normal;

besides, if they brood in a corner they will probably not adjust to reality. So Papa grabs Timothy, who is becoming maladjusted in a corner with an old violin, and forces him out into the playground to become normal. Timothy, who might have become a fine musician or a poet, which takes considerable solitude and an "offbeat" temperament, is forced into being a poor mixer and a woeful athlete.

What we forget, as amateur psychologists, is that Johnny is Johnny and Timothy is Timothy. They are not quite like any other children who ever entered the world before. They may be partly like Dad, or Mom, or more like Mom than Dad, or more like Aunt Sadie than anybody else, but they are most like Johnny and Timothy. There is a given individuality which cannot be expressed in terms of relations or generalities, nor done away with by fluctuations of the environment. You can say that Bert is a chip off the old block, but it is not a completely accurate saying. Bert is a new chip. He has his own peculiar grain, and you have to make allowances for it when you start whittling to make a little man out of him.

This is a fault of almost every book about child education that I have seen, including the various Sunday school textbooks. The material starts out by saying: "The children at this age are very dependent upon the assurance that the United States is here to stay," or something of that sort. But the experienced teacher knows that of the children in his class, only a fraction will conform to the established, pseudo-scientific pattern laid down by the textbook. I say "pseudo-scientific" because in the matter of human beings there is no accurate science except that which concerns the chemical, biological, and physical characteristics of man. And sometimes this is not any too accurate.

There is another thing to be remembered in these days when books on psychology for child-rearing are a dime a dozen, and flood every family book shelf. Some psychologists have impressed upon us the fact that Freddy is a delicate little mechanism, and that the least word rightly or wrongly chosen may affect his whole life—to say nothing of the wrong action. This has thrown many parents into a dither of fear, lest they ruin little Freddy's personality beyond repair.

On Saturday night Mom wants Freddy to go to bed, so that he can have his ten hours sleep, but also so that he will be out of the way for the party Mom and Pop are going to throw with the Joneses. Mom knows that Freddy would be a nuisance, sprawled all over the living room, and surrounded by all kinds of juvenile equipment for making noises and causing adults to fall down. She wants him to go to bed, and has suggested this desire in a kindly fashion. Freddy, however, doesn't take to the suggestion. He wants to see the Joneses. He has already peered into the refrigerator and seen the beer bottles, and he has an idea it's going to be a real party. He doesn't want to miss it. So he sits. Mom and Pop do not dare to do anything more than make a suggestion, for fear a harsh tone may turn little Freddy into a misanthrope before he's thirty-five. As for a lusty wallop across Freddy's behind, that is out of the question, because he might not understand and would be hurt emotionally as well as physically; it is possible that he might develop a black and blue mark, plus stomach ulcers from suppressed hatred, and a complex which might twist his whole being.

Psychology, or a misinterpretation of it, got us into this way of thinking. Actually a human being is a resilient cuss. A child may be as sensitive as a photographic plate, but he is much more adaptable and self-reliant. It takes a lot of doing or undoing to break a human being. If children were as tender and malleable as we sometimes think, very few would grow up to be anything but trembling

idiots. God takes care of drunks and small children
. . . as the saying goes. We ought not to overlook
the character that is given, the personality that
comes with each individual. Johnny, in spite of our
best efforts, may turn out to be an unmanageable
hoodlum. And Tommy, whose parents are out
every night and pay no attention to his development, may turn out to be a philosopher.

We do not have the lives of our children completely in our power. What a good thing that is.
Child-raising, like everything else, takes a good deal
of faith; and it is often true that every parent has
to guess about the best course of action to follow.
Should I spank Johnny or not? Should Susie go to
the dance with Jimmy or not? Is this a time for
leniency or harshness? Who ever knows with complete assurance? The parent has to make the best
decision he can and leave the rest to Johnny, Susie,
and God. A parent is something like an umpire;
most of the time, he has to "call 'em as he sees 'em,"
and stop worrying about it. Johnny may have been
called out when he was safe; but Johnny will re-
cuperate from the injustice, and will probably live
to score a run some other day.

I recall a wonderful scene in a movie called *Sit-
ting Pretty*. A squalling brat is throwing cereal

around the kitchen, and everyone has been too tender to do anything about such tantrums for fear of maiming the little baby's personality. Then Clifton Webb takes the bowl of cereal with a firm grip and crowns the baby with it, in a triumphant and decisive gesture. Baby stops crying. Baby, in spite of this act of adult aggression, will probably not grow up to be a monster.

With this much by way of meandering introduction I should like to generalize a bit about certain stages in the lives of children, which it may be of help to remember. I generalize with assurance, in the fashion of the time, for all educational manuals I have seen indulge in just such generalizations.

In the life of the child, there is first of all the Garden of Eden; an earthly paradise, no longer available in any way to adult manhood. But there is a sense in which very small children have a taste of this Garden of Eden. They live for a time in a miraculous world, accepted as it is with wonder and delight. The world is bathed, as G. K. Chesterton said, in a clear definite light. A drunk rolling down the street is neither good nor bad, but simply funny. A red apple on the ground in frost-time is a good thing, no matter whose apple it is; and it is accepted in its entirety of shape, color, feel, smell, taste.

Stories of princesses and kings are accepted for what they are without much confusion of shadow and substance. A pig is a pig, and nobody has to discourse on the pig's commercial value, for a small child to admire its rotund vulgarity.

I do not have so clear a memory of my childhood years, but I can recall a world that was wonderful and bright; it was a whole kind of place, and I never doubted its essential goodness or purpose. Even the sorrows and the pains of childhood (no less intense because they are of short duration) seem to fit into an acceptable pattern of a meaningful, miraculous world, peopled with giants and dwarfs, seen and unseen realities, red apples, toys, Santa Claus, cherubim and seraphim, and God.

Some of you who read this book may be parents of children who are still in the Garden of Eden. It is a responsibility of parents, in a Christian family especially, to remember this wondrous and unmoral quality of childhood, and to respond, as much as possible, with childlike eyes and perceptions, to this whole and splendid world. Unfortunately, we adults become speedily moral, crafty, jaded, and dull to the wonders of creation. Frequently we read back into the Garden of Eden ideas and disciplines, punishments and rewards, which have no meaning there, and which confuse the natural growth of little Adam and little Eve. Parents sometimes treat as sinful an action which for a small child has no possible quality of morality in it.

You may remember that delightful story about Mary McCoy, who went running into the garden one summer evening at twilight. In a little while she came back to the house. "Oh, Mummy," she said, with great excitement, "there's an elephant in the garden." Her mother, being adultly unimaginative, went into the garden and saw, in a dim corner beneath the trumpet vines, a gnarled and ancient stump, whereupon she chided Mary for telling a lie and sent her to her room to ask God's forgiveness. After a short while, little Mary came downstairs decked in a seraphic smile. "Did you ask God to forgive you for telling a story?" asked Mrs. McCoy. "Oh yes," said Mary, "God and I had quite a talk. I told him I was sorry that I thought I saw an elephant in the garden, but it was just an old stump." "Well?" asked the mother as Mary paused. Mary looked up and smiled. "God said, 'That's quite all right, Miss McCoy. I thought it was an elephant myself.'"

Surely part of the task of a Christian parent is to be sensitive to the life in the Garden of Eden; to try to retain the child's clarity of perception; to avoid pedestrianism, and to be a person who can share with the child something of the child's insight and delight in the dew-fresh world. Since the child is an individual he has his rights; and he has a right to the life in this Garden of Eden with its elephants, its Santa Claus and guardian angels and ridiculously sculptured pigs, its miracle of fields of buttercups.

There are adults who would take away this time of make-believe and fairyland; but they sin against childhood when they do. There is no more reason for a little child to accept the unimaginative perceptions of adults than there is for the same little child to be able to play golf in the low eighties, or to earn a living in Wall Street.

The next stage in a child's life might be called his adventure in the "watered garden . . . whose waters fail not" (Isaiah 58:11). This is the age of Tom Sawyer; or in modern terminology, the age of the little monsters—from about seven up to twelve.

Satan has been discovered, but he is not yet a formidable foe. He is a kind of necessary obstacle in the life of adventure and heroism, and his powers can be overcome as his character can be discerned. This is a garden in which there is some clear distinction between good and evil; and for the average, normal child, brought up in the morality of the public school and the bourgeois home, goodness always triumphs in the end.

It is a wonderful age, when the world has lost some of its freshness but none of its danger. An age of six-gun battles and air-rifle wars, stolen candy, broken heads, broken windows, and buckets of blood both real and imaginary. Eden is not quite lost; Satan is not known in his full panoply of power. The unexciting people are ministers, teachers, most parents, and stupid adults who never go fishing, play baseball, carry guns, catch tadpoles, or tear flies to pieces. The resources of craftsmanship and demonic ingenuity are inexhaustible. One moment of boredom and the battle is on, the tire empty of air, the river waded, the clothes torn to shreds, the body bruised and battered from a thousand valiant dyings in the sun. The little gardens whose waters fail not. Human individuals on the way to manhood, learning of risk, heroism, and adventure with a flamboyant faith that no matter how mighty are the powers of Satan, they are no match for Roy Rogers and the U. S. Marines.

Again it is a somewhat undutiful parent who fails to try, at least in imagination, to live again this glorious and perilous age, and to recognize that ten-year-old Johnny has a right to live through its splendors. Assuredly safeguards have to be taken, for it is a dangerous age. Yet I have never known a man whose parents denied him a large measure of freedom in this age of battle, who did not show the marks of incompleteness. Keep the ten-year-old out of the muddy street and the top of the tree, tie him to the apron string, and he will turn out to be a timid man, who has not learned how to give and take in the rough tumble of the world.

This appears to be that period of life when a good deal can happen to mold a member of the family. As parents, we have to learn to see the real importance of dirt, blood, football, Superman, and the horse-opera on television. It is a time of heroes and hero-worship. In religious matters the Jesus Tender Shepherd tradition in art, music, and story has to be replaced by a more robust tradition: the Carpenter, the strong Man, the unbroken King upon His cross.

The Christian family as a whole would have a richer life if parents could remember that children at every stage of their development have something to contribute. What they contribute at this stage is the knowledge (which adults often forget) that knighthood ought still to be in flower; that cowboys exist, murderers and bandits lurk behind every hedgerow, not to be feared but to be conquered.

This garden also is too temporary. Youth finds its way into another garden, also mentioned in the Bible. The garden with "a spring shut up, a fountain sealed" (Song of Solomon 4:12).

There is an abrupt change from one garden to another almost overnight. The voice cracks, the pimples appear, the body shoots up like a bean stalk, the eye becomes listless, dull, self-conscious, hiding the inward turmoil. This is the garden of adolescence. It is often a stagnant, smothered garden, for Satan has been discovered in all his overwhelming power, and he brings with him into the young heart anxiety and guilt, known and unknown.

The shock is one which some people never get over. The child's garden of delight, the boy's garden of rushing waters, becomes a garden of dreams and demons in half-light. The struggle of Michael and Satan, the very tragedy of living becomes localized in a place too small—the human heart. The soul is plowed by opposing forces, the whole person stands in arrested motion, his talents stifled into inactivity, his mind and spirit congested. Reality is confused with fantasy, visions with day-dreams.

So does the adolescent, appearing dull to the observer, look inward to behold the raging fires which he knows not how to quench. Having the devil in himself, he discerns his work in others and broods about it. Having dreamed of romance, grace, and purity, he ceaselessly worships that which he cannot find within himself, the strength, the confidence, the goodness of some Galahad. He is a great contradiction to himself and to his friends. He lurks in the basement telling smutty stories, and then lolls in languor upon the purifying sands. He exhibits a great outpouring of physical and emotional energy in sports, which brings perhaps forgetfulness to the broken dream within, and a sense of heroic accomplishment. Perhaps it is no wonder in this sad and curious time that the boy shows up as a pimply acolyte, and the girl a sexy little flirt.

I suppose this is the hardest age of all to deal with wisely. It is most difficult to understand, and most difficult for us to remember in our own lives, perhaps because we also took so small an enjoyment in it, so confused a look upon it.

Speaking very personally, as I look back upon my high school days, and at least a major part of my time in college, I do so with almost a shudder. There must have been, there were indeed happy times. But I am sorry to say they are half-sunken in a sea of vague, oppressive doubt and uncertainty; of fear, guilt, anxiety, and loneliness.

A Christian family is one which has some remembrance of this schizophrenic stage of life, and some tenderness and wisdom in dealing with those who live in this "garden . . . shut up, a fountain sealed." I imagine the most effective teaching during this period is not, strictly speaking, teaching at all; the youth will be taught, without a word being spoken, by those parents who have themselves passed beyond this garden shut up, and found some reservoirs of strength which will signify that they, having passed through this valley, still stand by the side of St. Michael.

I suppose this means that Christian parents will be those who have known not only these three gardens but another: the Garden of Gethsemane. This is the garden in which a man learns to admit that Paradise is gone forever from this earth, yet that it can be held in the memory to sweeten and make more vivid the real world. It is the garden in which man learns that the make-believe battle, the inevitable victory of the time of boyhood, must be replaced, not by battles won, but by the admission of a kind of perpetual defeat.

Certainly a man has to admit that he has lost his

gallant boyhood—but it is not necessary to lose the spirit of adventure, the zest for living. It is possible to learn to accept whatever conflict occurs with a faith in the eventual outcome of justice. Gethsemane is that garden in which we face Satan in all his might and deadly magnetism, and come out free from bondage to his strength—not by works, but by faith; not by conquest, but by forgiveness.

Each man's Gethsemane is different. One man struggles with his greed, another with his lust, another with his anger, all with their selfishness. Each man has different opponents to face: pain, grief, loneliness, monotony, danger. But the way out of this garden is the same for all. It is through faith in God's healing, God's redemption. There is no Christian family without that faith. And by that faith we, as parents, are brought to a greater knowledge of the necessities of our children; of their need for love, for discipline, for knowledge, and for our participation in their experience and in their problems, however great or small these problems may be.

Our real purpose in the world is to nurture those we have brought into the world. Of this nurture, providing food and clothing and shelter is but a part. The children are not just bodies, they are also souls; individuals with a right to "life, liberty, and the pursuit of happiness" from babyhood up. This right can only be properly exercised through our help. It is a help which demands of us a fresh memory of the ways of childhood, a good deal of imagination, a mountain of patience, a sea of understanding; and, as we say, it takes a world of time. What can be more important than attending to this culture? For we know that neither parents nor children can attain to the fullness of life except they learn of it from God.

I believe it is only when parents attend to this cultivation of the young that they begin to find a deepening devotion toward each other. And through this continuing cultivation, the love which can bind a family inseparably together begins to be known.

Sometimes situations arise which even the love and care of children by their parents cannot overcome. Loving your children is not the easy answer to a happy home life. But no home is blessed unless the love of parents goes out in infinite care to the children and returns from them fifty and a hundred fold. When this happens all the members of a family become tangled in a net of reverence and concern for each other within which the inevitable sorrows and losses will be more deeply felt, and yet more nobly accepted.

Surely one of our greatest mistakes in these days is that we consider the physical health of our children so important and neglect their growth of mind and spirit. Actually it is relatively easy to keep the children physically wholesome. Too often we suddenly see them grown up, blooming specimens of Venus and Adonis, with heads empty of great thoughts, spirits empty of earnest prayer. "For what shall it profit a man, if he shall gain the whole world, and lose his own soul?" (Mark 8:36)—and, we might add, through the carelessness of his parents.

Chapter 6

THE LIFE OF THE CHRISTIAN FAMILY

CHURCH leaders, including the clergy, have a lot to say about the Christian family, and most of the words they say are good, and worthy to be heard. But in some of the official talk about the Christian family and religion in the home, two mistakes are made.

First, Churchmen often assume that religion is entirely a formal sort of thing, exclusively connected with ecclesiastical life. The very phrase "religion in the home" seems to mean to many Christians the custom of family prayers, grace before meals, pictures of Jesus on the walls of the nursery, pictures of Gothic cathedrals on the walls of the den, and Bible stories at bedtime. All other home activities are relegated to a profane or secular category.

The second mistake follows from the first. The Church, meaning here of course its interested spokesmen, evidently believing that a church building is the only really adequate place for religion, and that ecclesiastical patterns of religious life are the only ones that God recognizes, has failed to make clear to people how ubiquitous God is.

William Temple once said, "It is a mistake to think that God is exclusively or even primarily interested in religion." God is interested in life. And He follows His interests with all the enthusiasm, I suspect, of a twelve-year-old following the fortunes of his favorite baseball player; no doubt more.

I should like to speak of certain family activities at this point, and I do so within this context: that religion is involved with these activities whether we are accustomed to think so or not, whether or not we recognize the overtones and undertones of religion. Perhaps the best way to say it is that God is involved in these activities. He is more important than religion.

A Christian family has some relationship with work. It is becoming increasingly rare to find all the members of a family engaged in a common enterprise. Even on the farm, what with modern farming methods and a growing discontent with rural life, it is quite likely that Dad and the tractor, with the help of one son or a hired man, do the work. In time past everybody in the farm family had his or her chores; the work was done by the whole family.

Certainly in most cases today Father does the work of supporting the family, and it is often true that Mother and the children do not even understand the kind of work he does. They have little share in his work, and frequently no interest in it. He works somewhere in an office at a task which nobody can describe with precision, and which may be so complex and specialized that hardly anybody is interested in its description. This means that Father has very little outlet at home for expressing his thoughts, ambitions, and desires about his work. His frustrations during the day or the month or the year may be closed up within him. It is difficult to share the problems that perplex him, the dreariness he has had to endure, or the triumphs, small as they may be, which he has won.

Furthermore, since the husband is out of the house all day, and quite generally a nincompoop about the management of the modern home, it is hard for him to understand the enthusiasm of his wife concerning her daily victories over the obstinate machines and gadgets of her kitchen, her defeats at the side of the washing machine, her frustrations brought on by the monstrous perversity of Venetian blinds. Father simply doesn't know what life is like when the vacuum cleaner begins to exhale dust, the automatic dryer goes up in smoke, the cat falls into the dishwasher, and the breadman comes to the back door just as the phone rings.

There isn't much to be done about this separateness of work short of Christian patience and understanding, except to recognize that the old unity of the home is broken up, so that it becomes essential for a family to have some home interests together, other than breadwinning work.

There are many families that have found a new interest in living and a new sense of the dignity of labor by some corporate enterprise on a vegetable garden or a summer cottage. One family that I know got together in a frenzy of varied activity while building a boat in a garage. I don't know whether the boat ever got out of the garage, but the project of building it seemed to be extremely beneficial to the unity of the family.

Various hobbies and crafts are also means of bringing families together to share with each other various interests and the handiwork of various talents. A family that just sits and looks at itself is likely to get bored no matter how much the members may love one another. If Dad likes wood carving, let him go in for that, while Mom scrapes down the old sideboard, Junior builds model airplanes, and Sis learns how to hemstitch. Such enterprises are therapeutic. They are excellent outlets for dammed-up energies and creative desires which are not possible to express through a ledger-book or an ironing board. And it is remarkable how various talents, once exercised, can dovetail and bring about an unexpected unity of interest. It is surely easier to share in one another's handiwork in these artistic and craftsmanlike avocations than in the professional work a man does in his business, or a woman does in the kitchen.

In spite of a snide remark about folk dancing, a few chapters back, I believe families ought to play together. As a medicine for harried nerves and frustrated emotions, play is even better than work; though one must add, of course, that the work a man does in his garden or basement shop may be play for him.

Play is good not only for the body, but for its own sake—any kind of play, from golf to charades. Some of the happiest memories of my life go back to the times when my father and mother gathered us children together, usually on Sunday evenings, to entertain ourselves. We had some music, all of us being dusted with enough talent to play some instrument, or to sing with sufficient accuracy so that we could recognize the tunes; and after that we played a game: checkers, hearts, Guggenheim, Monopoly, and such. We even tried Mah Jongg; twice, I think. I believe our most popular games were those which allowed us to sit or lie down on various pieces of furniture (all of us being naturally lazy) while we tried to use our minds. The game really didn't matter so much. We always argued and sometimes fought before the evening was over, disturbing the Sabbath calm. But we also laughed and forgot our isolated problems; and we discovered a union of interest which helped us to know each other and to bind us into a family. I can honestly say that, having known this side of family life, I rejoice that I grew up before television entered the American home.

Of course, what I am saying applies equally to outdoor recreation. I have met God at a baseball game, speaking subjectively, almost as often as I have met Him in church. God likes play, I feel certain, provided it is sincere and wholesome play. It would be good for Christian families to play together more often and more wholeheartedly; both games for children and games for adults. A family learns of affection, sacrifice, devotion, and fidelity not out of books so much as from shared experience. And in its work and play it learns of God's presence in every good aspect of human life. He is not a God who remains aloof and far off. He is not a God who restricts His revelation of Himself to people who are in church on Sunday morning. Mysteriously, subtly, continually His Spirit floods our lives, and sometimes dimly, sometimes clearly, we apprehend His life as we are at work in a garden, or playing with children in the autumn leaves, and rejoice that He has come to be with us as we work and play.

To be sure, our awareness of the Holy Spirit is not constant, and we need definite times and specific patterns and rituals so that we can consciously turn our attention to God to listen to Him, not leaving our response to random and fitful moments of sensitivity. Therefore, we ought to be specifically religious in the home, being careful to remember that we are not to try to make a home into a church.

Christian families ought to "say grace" before meals. Christian families ought to have family prayers at some regular and appointed times; in theory, at least once a day. In fact, however, family prayers seem to be a thing of the past, and I am not confident that we can restore the custom in our present day.

The nature of modern life is such that family prayers seem to be neither quite natural nor, from the standpoint of time, quite practical. My family used to have family prayers, but we got out of the habit somehow; not, I think, because my father lost interest or became less devout, but simply out of expediency.

Fathers punch time clocks and run for trains from suburbia to the cities, children have to catch buses to school, the "going to bed time" of urban society, and even of rural society, is much later than it once was. Evening meetings for parents who are community- and church-minded are a dime a dozen. People sleep later in the morning, and eat less breakfast, and are generally in more of a hurry. This is a great misfortune. But I think that family prayers, except for children at bedtime (when too often it amounts to the most innocent member of the family praying for the others) will not come back into general custom until the people increase greatly in piety, and the tempo of our culture changes. I confess that my own family, undirected by their father, has slipped into a very inadequate pattern in this respect.

Families ought surely to have times of Bible readings for the children; Bible stories for little tots, the Bible itself as they grow older. We ought to read the Bible ourselves, not unintelligently beginning at the beginning with a grim determination to go through all of it at any cost, but with some proper guide which any pastor can suggest to his people. If we are "on our own" we can at least read the Gospels, the Psalms, the Book of Job, the Books of Samuel, Ecclesiastes, and a few others without getting bogged down in Jewish food laws no longer applicable to us, and without the urgent necessity of a commentary to make sense of what we are reading.

The truth of the matter is not that the Bible is exceptionally difficult to read, but that *all* reading is becoming difficult, except the captions under pictures in *Life* and the ads in the weekly magazines. But that is another story.

We should have some religious pictures on the walls of the homestead. But here let me issue a warning. Some of the so-called religious art to which children are exposed at home and in church may do more harm than good in its teaching. Insincere, sloppy "hack work" masquerading as religious art simply because the subject matter is biblical or ecclesiastical is an affront both to art and religion.

The major output of the ecclesiastical publishing houses in the matter of religious pictures and of the Protestant Sunday school supply houses (not to mention the "Bleeding Heart" school of the Roman Catholics)—this vast output of sentimental, incompetent, insincere, and irreligious art should be dumped into Chesapeake Bay, or its equivalent.

When I speak of religious art that is good for home decoration I mean good reproductions of Rembrandt and Leonardo and Giotto and other classics, or some good etchings or woodcuts of themes having to do with the Christian religion and the life of faith.

If you are one of those people who says "I'm no art critic, I just know what I like," I beseech you not to inflict your uninstructed prejudices on your children. Let them grow toward maturity of aesthetic perception. Go and talk to the art expert in your community—there must be one somewhere around—and get his advice about good religious paintings. The real point is not that the children should completely understand everything they see, including paintings, but that they should grow up in a home in which the noble thoughts of great men of art, men of devout faith as well as of competent technique, surround them and become a part of their experience.

I will add a kind of footnote to this matter. There are many paintings which have stirred men's imaginations through the centuries. They can be purchased relatively cheaply in fine color reproductions, and this includes the work of many twentieth-century artists. Hang some of these on your living room walls, or even over the crib, for many of them have more religion in them than all the Sunday-school-pamphlet art laid end to end. Let me be specific. I would rather my children grew up surrounded by El Greco, Giotto, Cézanne, John Marin, Epstein, Lauren Ford, Chagall and Co., than by the entire religious output of the small-time illustrators who draw "Gentle Jesus Meek and Mild" for lesson leaflets. (Let me except the artists who are doing some imaginative things for some of the newer Church School courses, even though they seem to be straining unduly to accomplish their ends.) The small-time hacks who draw Jesus on the slopes of Galilee on Sunday are the same hacks who draw Jennie with the wind-blown skirt for the punchboard-calendar decorations of America on Monday—only the Sunday school "art" is less competent.

Part of our difficulty may be that we are infected with the Ralph Adams Cram virus. A distinguished professor of history once remarked that Cram was the most pernicious influence on American art of the twentieth century. He made popular, especially among Episcopalians, the notion that good religious art and architecture was of one type, which flourished several hundred years ago. On that assumption one goes ahead through changing scenes, climates, and cultures and does copy work. Copy work in architecture is the Episcopalian's notion of a proper church. Copy work in painting is his notion of good Christian art.

What I have said about paintings in the home applies to music also. Many families do not "make their own music," as they once did, and few hold a Sunday evening hymn sing around the piano. But almost all families these days own some kind of record player, often a very good hi-fi set; and I would suggest that it is a responsibility of Christian parents to see that some of the music played in the home is religious music. I do not mean by religious music that which has an obvious ecclesiastical content, such as a "hymn for the day," but that which has been composed through the centuries by men of spiritual insight and Christian devotion.

The music from television and radio is, by and large, of two types: (1) the popular classics and (2) jazz (or what is infinitely worse, rock-and-roll). As far as religious music is concerned the best that can be expected is a sentimental hymn. But there is a huge library of good music available on records, all the way from plainsong to Hindemith and Paul Creston, which speaks of man's spiritual desire and religious experience. Some of it is ecclesiastical—music written for church performance. Some of it is "concert-hall music," and yet witnesses profoundly to the reality of the supernatural, and to the searching thirst of man for a redemption not possible on this earth. This music should be played in our homes. In fact, our children should grow up surrounded by these harmonies, melodies, dissonances, sounds. Among all the other avenues there are, this is truly a Champs Élysées, along which we absorb even unknowingly the winds of life.

If we have a record player (to say nothing of hi-fi), we ought to have, besides the popular classics and the stacks of Benny Goodman and Tommy

Dorsey, the Bach B minor Mass, some of the excellent church music of the Mormon Tabernacle choir, some Mozart and Rachmaninoff, and madrigals of the Randolph Singers, and something of Biggs and Schweitzer on the organ, and if possible Honegger's *Le Roi David*—a whole host of magnificent and inspiring compositions which will remind us and our children that man does not live by bread alone; which will remind us that from the beginnings of time man has expressed something of his otherworldly desire and his undemonstrated hope by way of music.

A further possibility of fostering the Christian religion in the home is in the commemoration of Church holidays, and even some "secular" holidays.

I have always been deeply grateful to my parents for the care they took to emphasize the importance of great days and seasons of the Church Year. This is another matter which the modern family seems to deal with less wisely than families of an earlier generation. Certain elaborate family rituals were performed in our home at such times as Christmas, Thanksgiving Day, Easter, which have left me with indelible and cherished memories, which I believe made these holy days more sacred, although the rituals were in themselves not always ecclesiastical.

There were certain things to be done on Christmas Eve, and certain times for doing them; certain formalities to be observed even when we were very young. We always wrapped our own gifts, and wouldn't think of having them wrapped by a wrapping expert in a store. (What an abominable custom! To dress up the symbol of love and sacrifice by a person who cares nothing about the person to receive the gift!) We were not allowed to have the tree lighted until Christmas morning. We met together, my brother, sister, and I, at the top of the stairs, and waited in expectancy and tense anticipation until Father called out, "All right, come down now." Then with a clatter we were downstairs, and looked upon the tree together; it burst upon us in its myriad candle flame with mysterious and half-forgotten splendor.

The same thing is true (and was true for us) of other days. We were encouraged to take some time and patience to make things for others, that by our help the holiday or holy-day occasion might be something extraordinary, to be remembered with joy forever.

Some of these matters haven't much to do with

Church; but they have to do with family virtues. They have something to do with the care taken to make a Christmas card for sister, even when you think she is something of a brat; something to do with saving pennies to buy a jackknife for big brother who treats you like the repulsive little boy he thinks you are. These secular, human, family things involve trouble taken for each other, the mutual sharing of gifts, talent, handiwork. They involve the symbols and instruments of love, and in a natural kind of way are sacramental acts.

Because of these things done, these special occasions that are highlighted and raised up from the daily level of existence, a family makes itself more available to the intrusion of the supreme Guest: the living God.

I am always rather annoyed when I hear a parent say to a child, "Here, dear; here's five (or fifty-five) dollars for your birthday. Run downtown and buy something you like." I am always sorry for the family that gets too old to bother with a Christmas tree, or that brags that they do not make much of Easter. They are not even aware of the passing of the Fourth of July. But I have a naive, indeed perhaps too simple, feeling that God Himself must like to be with those who in mutual affection and gladness make much of august occasions, even though they may not open their ceremonies with the Collect for the day. It is in doing things together that understanding grows and all the members of the family school themselves in unselfishness, patience, and sacrifice. A family that does everything separately might have fewer skirmishes, tears, arguments, and major battles; but it is hardly a family.

I have tried to be personal in these discussions; I have not relied much on other authorities, indeed, not enough. I have spoken only of those things which I have known, and which I have found to be true or false, valuable or worthless.

I know that when I am most self-critical and most grieved about my own failures, it is the remembrance of love which was shown through "secular" occasions in the family in which I was raised which supports me, even more than the rules of Christian duties, or the remembrance of strictly religious activities. I do not think I am a complete pagan because of this. I believe the ground of man's apprehension of God is broader and deeper than we sometimes like to concede.

The Fourth of July in my family was a great day. We didn't begin shooting off fireworks in

June. We had to wait until the day itself. Then we had one long, rousing, cannonading blast of cap, cracker, candle, and skyrocket. It began at six in the morning, and ended at some late, dreadful hour of the night. We must have eaten something during the day, but I am not sure that we did. If we did I am certain it was eaten outdoors, or (if it rained) on the porch.

My father had an old muzzle-loading cannon which had been forged by my grandfather. It made a "BOOM" which could be heard from Oyster Bay, Long Island, all the way up the Connecticut shore to New London. My father alone was man enough to fire this monster cannon. When he did so, which was about four times during the day, we kids stuffed cotton in our ears; my mother, who was anti-cannon, retreated to the kitchen; and the collie went under the bed in the guest room. When that cannon went off with a resounding boom that echoed proudly down the bay, and when the smoke rose thick and blue over the garden, we knew that we were independent. Liberty was our birthright.

It was a tremendously secular day. But somehow at the close of it, considering the firecrackers loaned and given, the punk shared, the sympathy offered when a finger was burned—considering that under-

neath the trite and childish noise there was con-
veyed to us in some fashion the remembrance of
the time when men of stature rose in dignity for
the right to become men of responsibility—considering these things, there was a sacredness about
the day as well as a secularness. It was as though a
man might say, "Surely God is in this place though
I knew it not." He came not in answer to the noisy
summons of us children, but to be a Guest, a Com-
panion, in a place where His children were trying
to express something about the dignity of men, and
about their desire to escape from the yoke of bondage. For all I know God may have enjoyed the
noise of that cannon, and cried out "Hurrah"; because this cannon was aimed at no one, only at the
treetops and the sky beyond; its noise was a shout
of praise for courage, and the insatiable thirst of the
spirit after liberty under the skies of God.

Considerations of safety, and the laws of the
State, have outlawed for us in most parts of the
country the noisy Fourth, but the principles for
which it stood remain the same. Some equivalent
should be found; it is not enough to celebrate our
independence by sleeping late and watching television.

So may we work and play and worship together

in families. We ought to make use of every one of these forms and patterns of formal religion which fit naturally into the life of the home. These may become instruments of grace as well as the sacraments of the Church. Where parents and children work and pray and play together and attend to those things which demand care and sacrifice from all the members of the family, God cannot be far off. Within the shared sorrows, joys, common tasks, and uncommon occasions there are a thousand springs of the Holy Spirit. Suddenly we come to realize the source of the waters. And we learn again and again to say, "Surely God is in this place and I knew it not."

In such a home, the family is on its way to becoming Christian—a home where every sadness is relieved by faith, every sin by forgiveness, and every evil by love.

Chapter 7

FAMILY, CHURCH, AND GOD

I SAID at the beginning of this little book that I am no expert on the family, and that is by this time, I am afraid, completely apparent. I have no formulas to offer for the reconstruction of family life. People today, lured on, I suspect, by science, which has given us so many precise answers and exact formulas, have gone formula crazy. Because there is a formula for making plastic or penicillin, we begin to think there must be a formula for making Christian families. This hope for a non-failing solution amounts to faith in incantations and magic words. There are no formulas for marriage and the family, for these involve human beings, and human beings in their wholeness are (fortunately) unmeasurable. In human relations there are no exact equations; and no rules apply to every situation. Only the principles of Christ are applicable, such as "Repent ye, for the Kingdom of God is at hand," and "Thou shalt love the Lord thy God . . . and thy neighbor as thyself."

Even the specialist on the family will not give the formulas some people desire. A specialist might well have more precise knowledge than I about the present condition of the family, he might have deeper insight into the sexual side, or the spiritual side, or the economic or ecclesiastical sides of marriage; he might be much wiser than I about man and God and little children too. But whatever perception or knowledge may be his, he would still be without a formula to give you. If he told you he had one he would be a fraud.

About the best anyone can say is this: "Work out your own salvation in fear and trembling." Perhaps this sounds harsh, but what else would you have us say? Is anybody so romantic as to think that the reading of a few books on the subject of the Christian family will solve all family problems?

To work out one's own salvation in fear and trembling is the advice of St. Paul, and it is given in a context of Christian belief: the belief that nobody can work out any kind of salvation for anybody, including himself, without God.

The point is that no one can "solve your problem" except you and your family. All that others can do is to share their experience, their knowledge, and the things that have been real and redeeming for them. These you can add to your own resources. A family is a subjective, intimate, individualistic kind of thing, and no outsider can solve its problems.

I am strongly of the opinion that the most adequate solutions to family problems are to be found
by those who live within the community of Christ,
which is the Church. A family needs religion; it
needs God. But I do not think there is any vital
understanding of religion, nor any very meaningful
experience of God apart from the Church, the
community of believers which guards and trans-
mits the essential faith from one generation to
another and within its fellowship gives witness to
the reality and glory of the Lord.

The Church is a kind of roadside stand along
the highways of the human journey—a place of
rest and refreshment, where hungry souls are fed,
and the dry wells of the spirit are refilled.

The Church is an information bureau, also. The
place that keeps the official maps and guides, so to
speak, which have been wrought by the saints and
prophets and thinkers of the years. The Church is
the place where one may find out which journeys
are fruitless and which are filled with meaning. It
is the place to find out the shape of the world, to
discover which routes lead out into meaninglessness and which roads lead to life.

I may have given the impression, when speaking

of religion and theology, that I considered theology to be an unimportant kind of exercise for people who have nothing better to do. But let me repeat that theology is a necessary by-product of living religion. It grows out of man's awareness of God. It observes, and clarifies, and interprets the religious experience out of which it arises. Without the framework of theology, without creeds and the interpretation of creeds, religion would have no backbone; it would slump down into a formless mess of spiritual feeling. But theology is not an end in itself; its importance is that of the backbone: to keep the body upright; in this case, to hold firm and straight the body of Christian truth which men have experienced. It is theology that can teach men the paths to travel in order to discover in their own lives the unique and saving power of Christ which has been revealed through history.

So theology is essential, but let us remember that it is no substitute for the religious experience itself. The bones of a man are essential; and a skeleton gives us some notion of a man's shape. But a skeleton is no substitute for a living person.

The Church is a place for companionship, again like the roadside stand, where travellers and pilgrims gather for good fellowship and communion with one another "in the unity of the spirit and in the bond of peace." I have sometimes stopped in my journeys at those places which advertise "Truckers Welcome," and I have discovered that these professional burden bearers to the world have a rather admirable spirit of camaraderie. They stop at roadside stands not just for food and gas, but to exchange stories with their fellows and to find out the detours that lie ahead. They take a turn at the pinball machine, and "chew the fat" a while, and then go out into the world again with a "thumbs up" gesture, and a "Good luck, Joe" ringing in their ears. They have made their roadside stands a kind of church, albeit in a secular sense. They find companionship therein, to sustain them in their labors.

So the Church ought to be for us the place of friendliness and companionship in the spirit of Christ. Perhaps instead of our innocuous signs that read "Everybody welcome," we should put up signs that read "Christians welcome." Especially Christians, that they may know within this fellowship the communion of the spirit; and "the giant laughter of Christian men."

The Church should be for the family a community which includes all these things I have mentioned, for religion in the home is not enough. No matter how frequently or how richly God invades the life of the home, it is important that again and again we return to the Church where God has promised to be with us. We need to be strengthened, redirected, enlivened by participation in this larger family life, in the whole Family of God.

Through the habitual conformity to the Church's pattern of liturgy, through prayer, sermon, sacrament, our perceptions are sharpened, our knowledge of God deepened. God does intrude upon our lives here, there, and everywhere, and often His intrusion is quite unexpected. But this is not something that wise people count on too much. The more we learn of Him and come to know Him in His holy temple, the more clearly are we able to see His footsteps treading the paths of our common life in places where we did not expect to find Him. God apparently (in my experience more often than not) comes to visit in the home those who have discovered Him before His altar.

The Christian family is a churchgoing family. The Church rightly makes every effort to direct and nourish its families in special as well as in the habitual ways.

There are many techniques and devices in which the Church can be of help. Most of them you know.

In counselling before marriage, in its pastoral care of families, services for renewing of marriage vows, groups for young married couples, family dinners, family services, and other ways the Church seeks to give strength to families for the Christian life. As well as the regular services in which the family should take part, these other instruments the Church provides can aid us in keeping the family strong and active within the Family of God.

Perhaps I should mention here one pitfall into which the Church sometimes falls. Marriage is not a special privilege of Christians. It is of the divine order of creation, and the Church's responsibility for laws and ideals that should govern marriage extends only to its own membership.

It is not the Church's business to set down marriage and divorce laws for the whole society. What the State may legislate for marriages and grant as valid cause for divorce will never precisely coincide with the meaning of marriage to the Christian mind. We cannot legislate for society. We can hold to our ideal and legislate as we will for our own fellowship.

It seems reasonable to suppose that we Christians agree that marriage is an indissoluble bond between two people. We would not all agree, even within the Christian fellowship, as to the just causes for separation and divorce. It appears to some that in the New Testament the teaching of our Lord is clear and perfectly definite. It appears to others that His teaching on the subject not only refers to certain Jewish customs, and is therefore not applicable to every society, but also that there may be textual problems involved in the relevant passages which are not clear to us; and that the apparent legalism of Jesus' teaching on the subject is somewhat misleading. This is not the place for a complex discussion of the critical problems of the New Testament, even if I had the learning to do it. But I may state frankly my own position, which is that in this matter as in many others it is safer to base one's interpretation on the whole attitude and teaching of Christ, rather than on one or two specific statements as they appear in the Gospel records. If anything seems clear in the New Testament as a whole, it is that Christ treated persons as persons, and dealt with people as individuals. I happen to think that the legalistic idea of "no divorce except for adultery," and a prohibition on remarriage of divorced persons under any circumstances, are not congruous with the Gospel teaching in its wholeness. Since it is possible that we, or the men who wrote the Gospels, misinterpreted the mind of Christ, and conceivable that the principle upon which He dealt with individuals is broader than our interpretations of His illustrations of the principle, I would prefer to take a stand upon some position less legalistic. It is not a question therefore to my mind of making rules more strict or more lenient, as much as it is a question of whether we shall be determined to live by a rule-book of laws universally applicable, or by the spirit of the Lord, knowing that each human relationship, good or bad, must be treated on its own merits or demerits; and that forgiveness always goes beyond the law.

In marriage, in the life of the family, we all fail to some degree, and as in all other conditions of men, we must throw ourselves upon the divine forgiveness. Within this knowledge a Christian will admit that human love is wonderful but transient. All human love springs out of the need of one person for another. All human love has in it an erotic element. This means that all love needs sanctification, needs to be raised from *eros* to *agape*, in which we love not only with a desire to possess, and to satisfy our need, but for the sake of the other person, for what he is in himself as God's child.

Life within the Christian family is often very

difficult, as it is within non-Christian families. Every enterprise, every affection and desire, falls short of fullness and of health unless it is offered to God to be purified and blessed by Him. The life within any home requires patience and discipline, tenderness and courage, justice, fidelity, and understanding. These qualities are not possible for sinful man to achieve except he be overshadowed by the wings of the Lord. The Christian family is one in which all the members know, at least with some intuition though the knowledge never be articulated, that the divine love must take hold of the human love and transpose it into a new key.

Finally, the Christian family through its fellowship with Christ has a further goal and purpose beyond those of all other families. Sex is not the end of marriage, but the means to an end. Security and happiness are not the ends of marriage, but by-products of the adventure. The end of marriage, for a Christian, is the end of man: eternal life in the Family of God, in which "they neither marry nor are given in marriage," but abide in the joy of the Lord.

In this Christian hope the family can best accomplish its important and difficult functions. In this hope earthly tensions can be overcome, earthly failures and sorrows can be transformed. The worldly pleasures of the family can be gratefully enjoyed in their proper season, and relinquished when the time comes without bitterness or despair. The Christian family will be persuaded that neither death nor life, things present nor things to come, can separate it from God's love.